Light reflecting off a pool of rippling water

Water

Aaron Frisch

A+

Smart Apple Media

COPYRIGHT

Published by Smart Apple Media

1980 Lookout Drive, North Mankato, MN 56003

Designed by Rita Marshall

Copyright © 2002 Smart Apple Media. International copyright reserved in all countries. No part of this book may be reproduced in any form without written permission from the publisher.

Printed in the United States of America

Photographs by Craig Davis, KAC Productions (Kathy Adams Clark, Larry Ditto), Tom Myers, Tom Stack & Associates (Ken Davis, Ed Robinson)

Library of Congress Cataloging-in-Publication Data

Frisch, Aaron. Water / by Aaron Frisch. p. cm. — (Elements series)

Includes index.

ISBN 1-58340-076-1

1. Water—Juvenile literature. [1. Water.] I. Title. II. Elements series (North Mankato, Minn.)

GB662.3 .F75 2001   553.7—dc21   00-054172

First Edition 9 8 7 6 5 4 3 2 1

Water

CONTENTS

What Is Water?

Without water, there would be no life on Earth. The human body is about 65 percent water. Every other living thing is also made mostly of water. A grown-up needs to take in about eight glasses of water every day. Except for air, nothing is more critical for life. ⟳ Water is the most common substance on Earth. It covers more than 70 percent of the planet. Water is made of tiny particles called molecules. A single drop of water contains trillions of molecules. These molecules

Water moves constantly around the earth

are made up of hydrogen and oxygen. By themselves, hydro-

gen and oxygen are gases. But when they are combined, they

form water. ⌇ Most of the water on Earth is liquid. But it

can also be a solid (ice) or a gas (water **The Grand Canyon**

vapor). Water turns into ice when it is **was formed over**

millions of years as

the flowing water

32° F (0° C) or colder. Water turns into **of the Colorado**

River wore away at

vapor when it is heated up. As water **the earth.**

gets warmer, its molecules move around faster than normal.

Some of the molecules break free from the water and rise into

the air. This is why water turns into steam—hot water vapor—

when it is boiled. ⌒ When water is liquid, its molecules

stick together. This can be seen in the way water drips from a

faucet. It slowly stretches from the faucet, lets go, and snaps

Icicles form when dripping water freezes

Water vapor condenses into dew during cool nights

into a little ball of water. The force that holds water together

is called **surface tension**. The surface tension of water is

strong enough that some kinds of insects can walk across it,

making small dimples in the water but not sinking into it.

The Water Cycle

There is the same amount of water on Earth today as

there was billions of years ago. Most water is in the ocean. As

the sun shines on the ocean, some of this water **evaporates**.

This water vapor forms clouds. When it gets cold enough, the

vapor in clouds condenses—or forms into rain or snow—and

falls back to Earth. Eventually, all water finds its way back to

the ocean. In this way, water is never used up and never dis-

appears. It is simply **recycled**.

The amount of water on Earth never changes

Using Water

People use water for many things. In the United States, the average person uses more than 100 gallons (380 l) of water every day. This includes water for drinking, cooking food, washing clothes, showering, and flushing toilets. Farmers use water to irrigate their crops. Power plants boil water to make steam, which can be used to create electricity.

About 40 percent of all the water used in the United States is used by farmers to irrigate crops.

People also use water to swim and sail, and for doing other fun activities. About 97 percent of the water in the world is

in the ocean. Water in the ocean has salt in it. This is why it is

called saltwater. People can't drink saltwater or water their

crops with it. But there is a way to remove the salt from salt-

Almost all of the world's water is saltwater

water. First, the saltwater must be heated until it boils. As the

steam rises, it leaves the salt behind. The steam from the water

goes through a pipe and into a cool container. The steam then

condenses into freshwater, which people **Most of the world's freshwater is locked in glaciers and ice caps near the north and south poles.**

can use. This process is called distillation.

The same thing happens when seawater

evaporates and then falls back to the earth

as freshwater rain.

Rain helps to move water from the ocean to land

Water Quality

People get the water they use every day from lakes, rivers, or water under the ground. Often, this water is sent through pipes to treatment plants. There the water is purified, or cleaned, to get rid of any **bacteria** and bad tastes. Then the water is piped to homes and other buildings. The waste water from homes is called **sewage**. Sewage is usually piped back to treatment plants, where it is purified again. The water may be used again immediately or may be returned to a lake or river.

> **Most of the water we drink comes from lakes and rivers**

Water pollution is a big problem in many areas of the world. Water is polluted when people dump sewage, chemicals, oil, and other things into rivers and lakes. Water pollution can also be caused by smoke from factories and cars. This smoke rises into the air and combines with water vapor and rain. Many of the things in polluted water can make people sick. The world will always have water. But it is important that we keep this resource clean for future generations.

Americans pay about $1.30 for every 1,000 gallons (3,800 l) of water they use.

Oil spills are one of the worst forms of water pollution

Forms of Water

Water can be in three forms: ice, liquid, and gas. You can see it in all three forms with a simple experiment.

What You Need

Two ice cubes

A sealable sandwich bag

A microwave-safe plate

A microwave oven

What You Do

1. Put the ice cubes in the sandwich bag. Seal the bag shut and set it on the plate. Then set the plate and bag in the microwave.

2. Turn the microwave on at full power. Watch what happens. The ice cubes melt and become liquid.

3. Let the microwave keep running after the ice becomes liquid. Watch what happens in the bag now. Some of the liquid becomes steam and puffs the bag up. (Turn off the microwave when the bag starts to get full of air. Let the bag cool before you take it out.)

The water changes from ice to liquid to steam because it gets hot. When it gets hot, its molecules start to move very fast and spread out. This is why the water vapor makes the bag puff up.

Water changes in form from season to season

INFORMATION

Index

Words to Know

bacteria (bak-TEER-ee-uh)—tiny organisms; some of them cause diseases

evaporates (ee-VAP-uh-rates)—turns into a gas form called vapor

irrigate (EER-uh-gate)—to supply crops with water from pipes or ditches

recycled (ree-SY-kuld)—used again and again

sewage (SOO-edge)—waste water carried away from people's homes

surface tension (SER-fuss ten-shun)—the force that holds water molecules together

Read More

Richardson, Joy. *The Water Cycle*. New York: Franklin Watts, 1992.

White, Larry. *Water: Simple Experiments for Young Scientists*. Brookfield, Conn.:
    The Millbrook Press, 1995.

Wick, Walter. *A Drop of Water*. New York: Scholastic Press, 1997.

Internet Sites

Environment Canada: Fresh Water
http://www.ec.gc.ca/water/en/
nature/prop/e_prop.htm

USGS Water Science for Schools
http://ga.water.usgs.gov/edu/

The Groundwater Foundation
http://www.groundwater.org/